Pictorial Archive of
DECORATIVE
FRAMES & LABELS

550 Copyright-Free Designs

Edited by
Carol Belanger Grafton

Dover Publications, Inc.
New York

Published in Canada by General Publishing Company, Ltd., 30 Lesmill Road, Don Mills, Toronto, Ontario.

Pictorial Archive of Decorative Frames and Labels: 550 Copyright-Free Designs is a new work, first published by Dover Publications, Inc., in 1982.

DOVER *Pictorial Archive* SERIES

Manufactured in the United States of America
Dover Publications, Inc.
31 East 2nd Street
Mineola, N.Y. 11501

Library of Congress Cataloging in Publication Data
Main entry under title:

Pictorial archive of decorative frames and labels.

    1. Borders, Ornamental (Decorative arts) 2. Labels.
I. Grafton, Carol Belanger.
NK3630.4.B67P5   745.4   81-17532
ISBN 0-486-24277-3   AACR2

Publisher's Note

Carol Belanger Grafton has carefully selected this anthology of frames and labels from over thirty sources, most of them inaccessible to the general public. They range from typefounders' catalogues of the nineteenth and twentieth centuries to books such as *L'Imprimerie en France* and *Formenschatz*. Although labels and frames must by their very nature adhere to a certain form, designers and craftsmen are here treated to a tremendous variety, spanning styles as diverse as Renaissance and Art Nouveau and treating material (including florals and animal themes) that can lend itself to a wide number of projects.

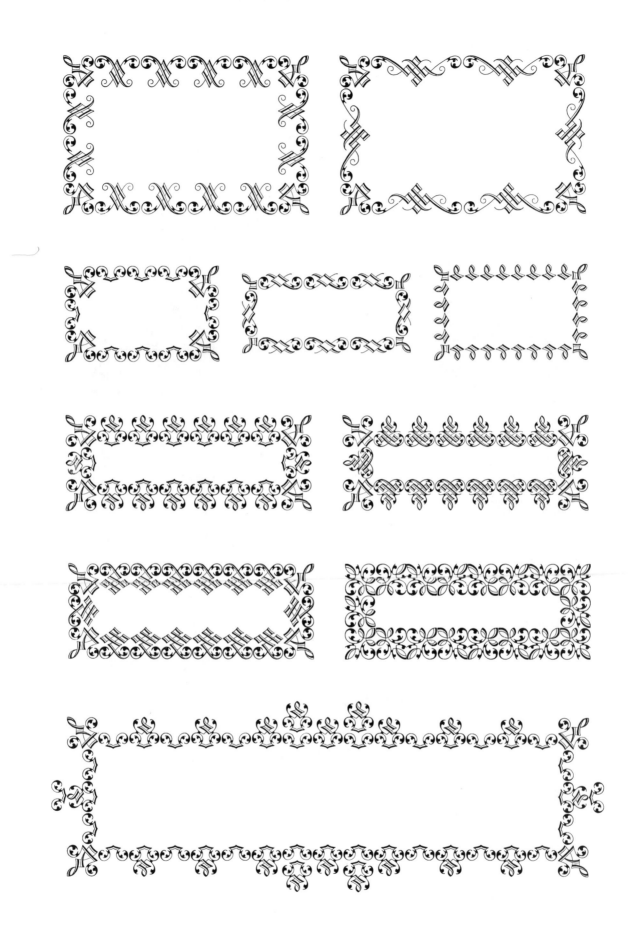

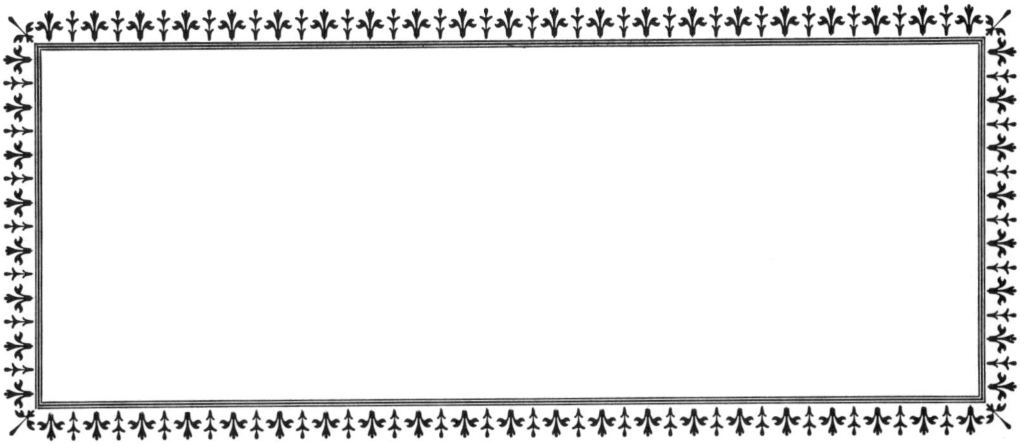

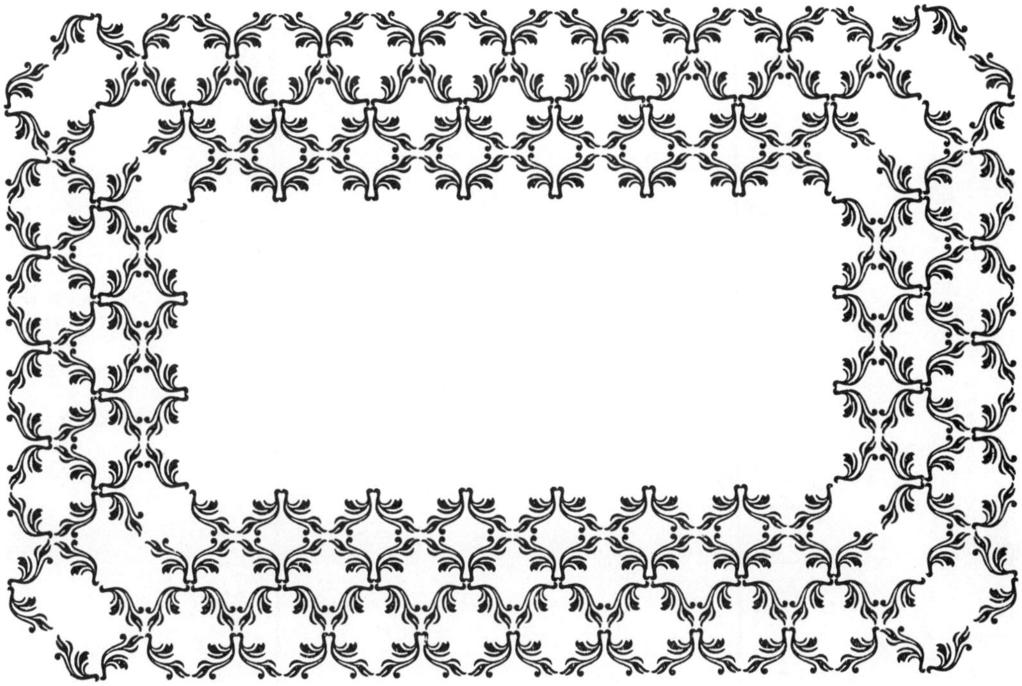

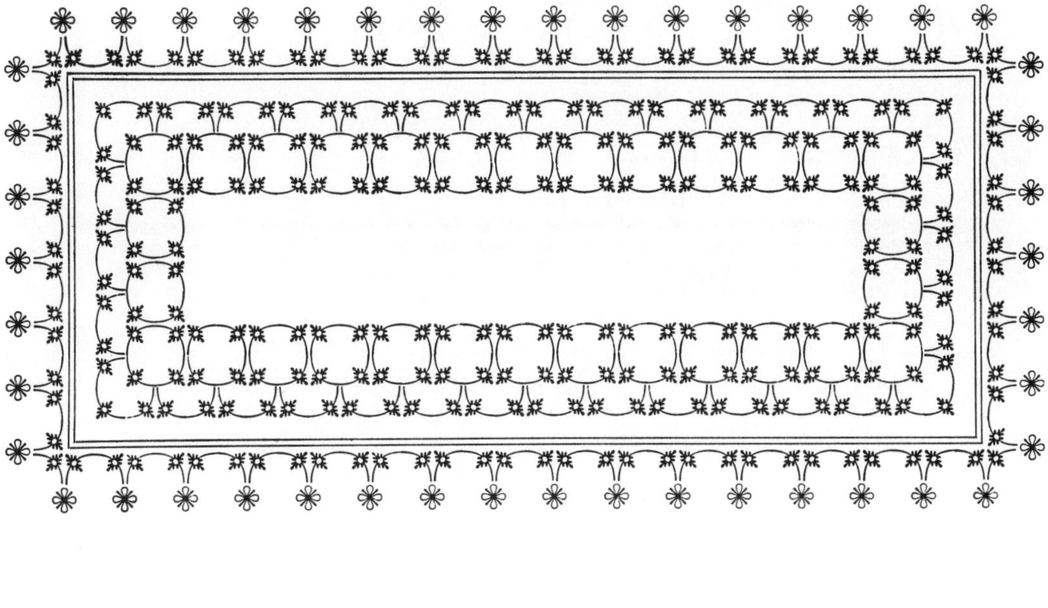

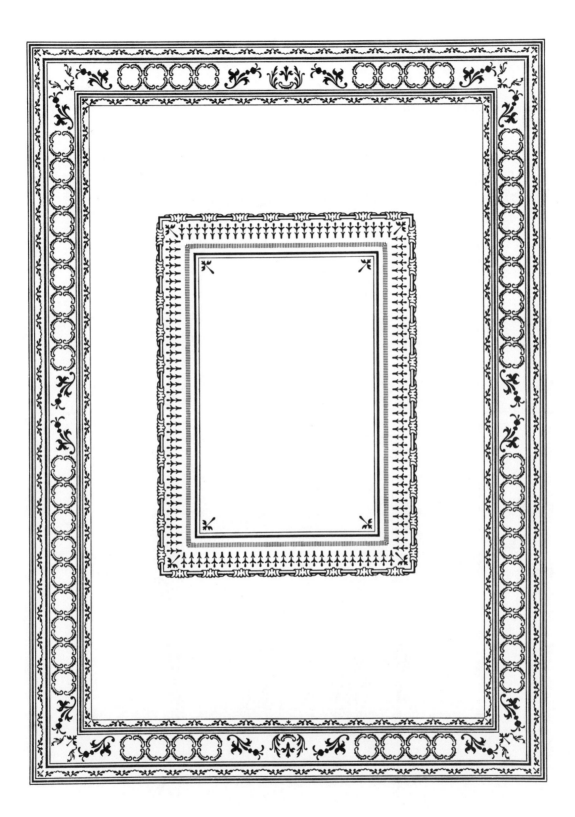

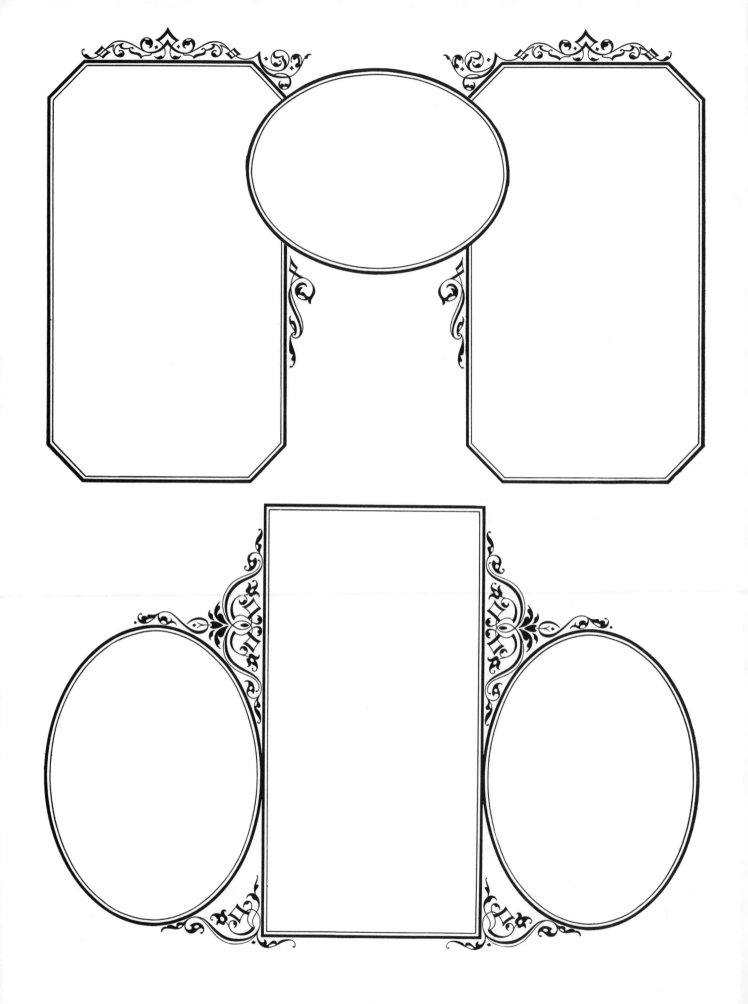

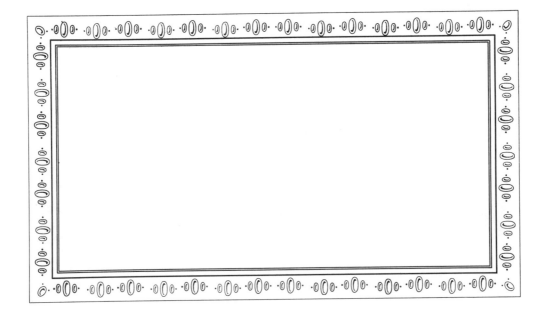

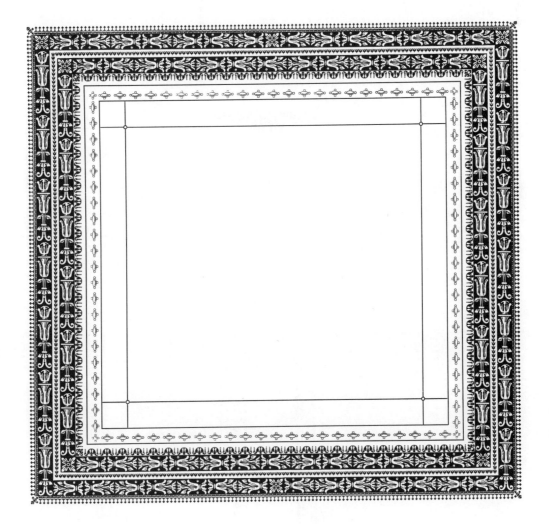

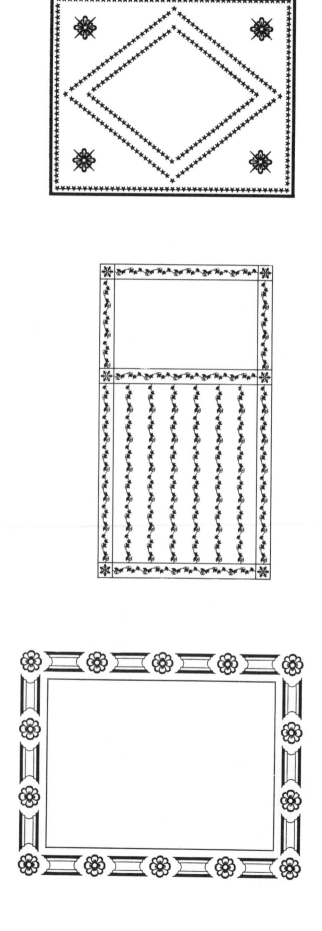

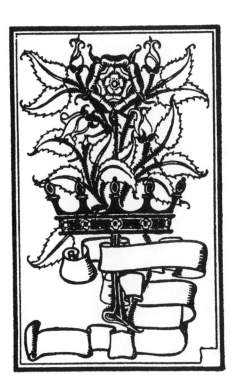

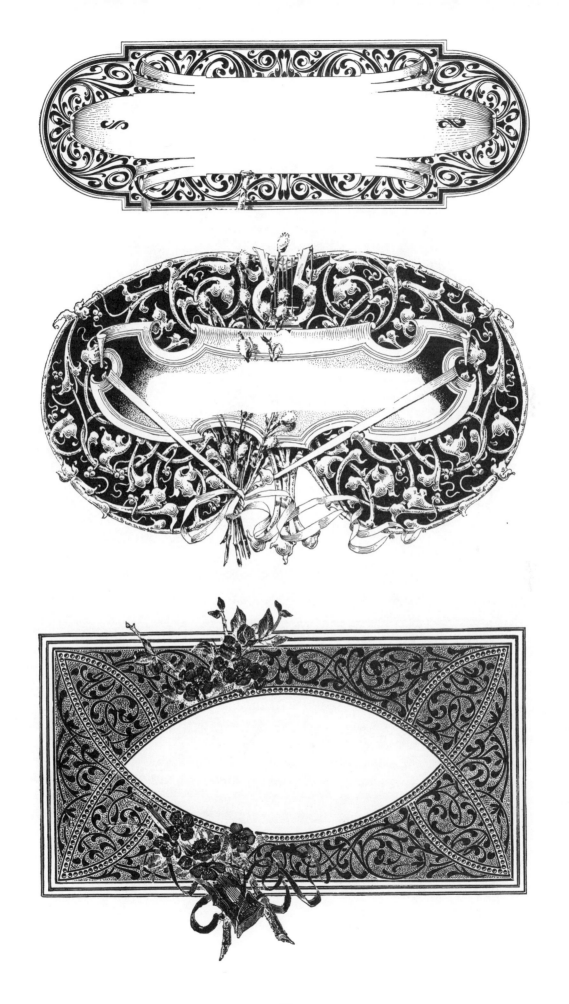

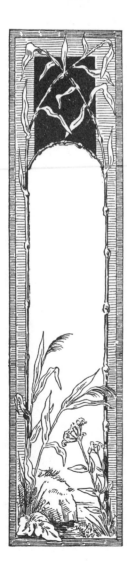

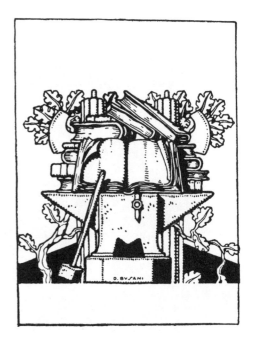

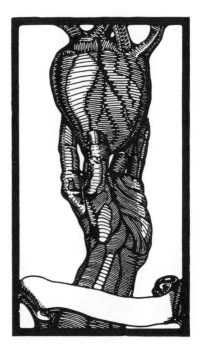

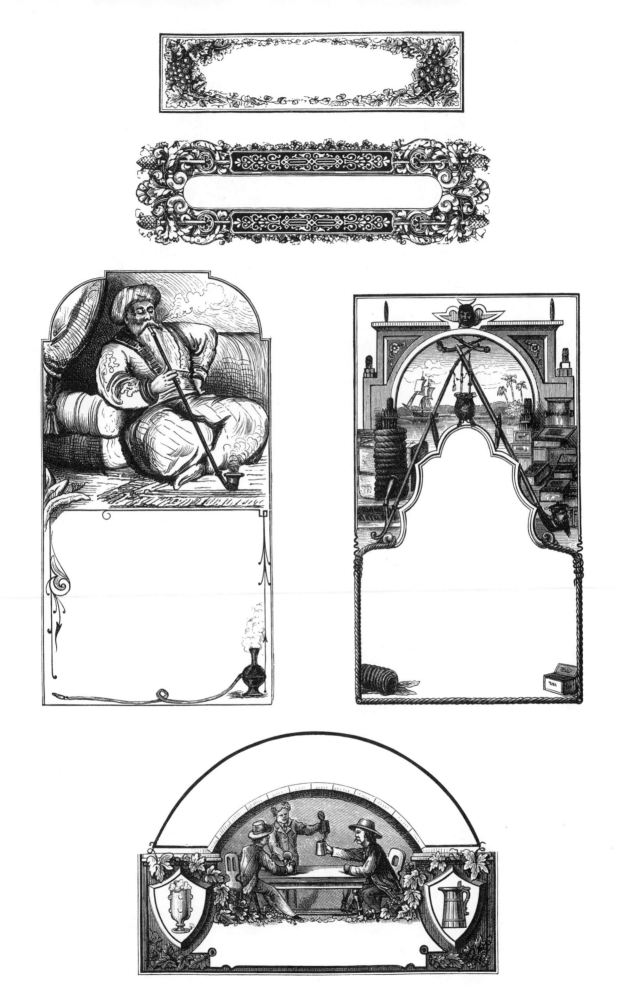

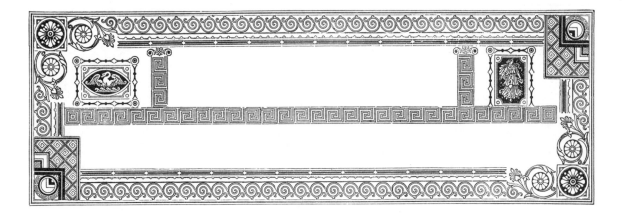

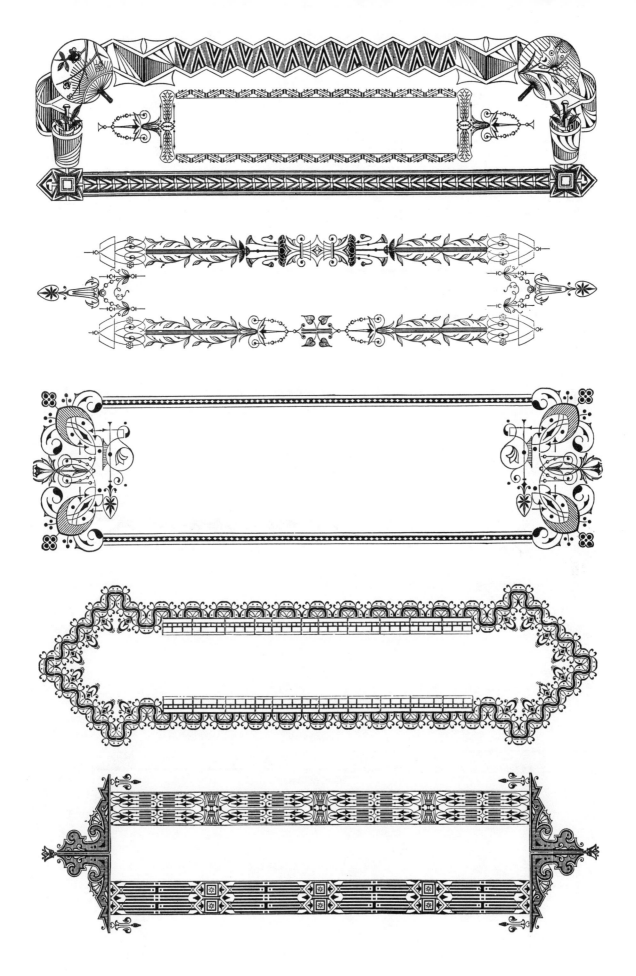

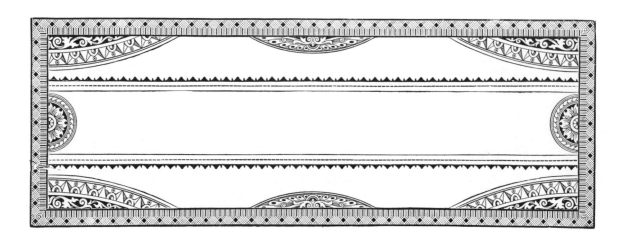

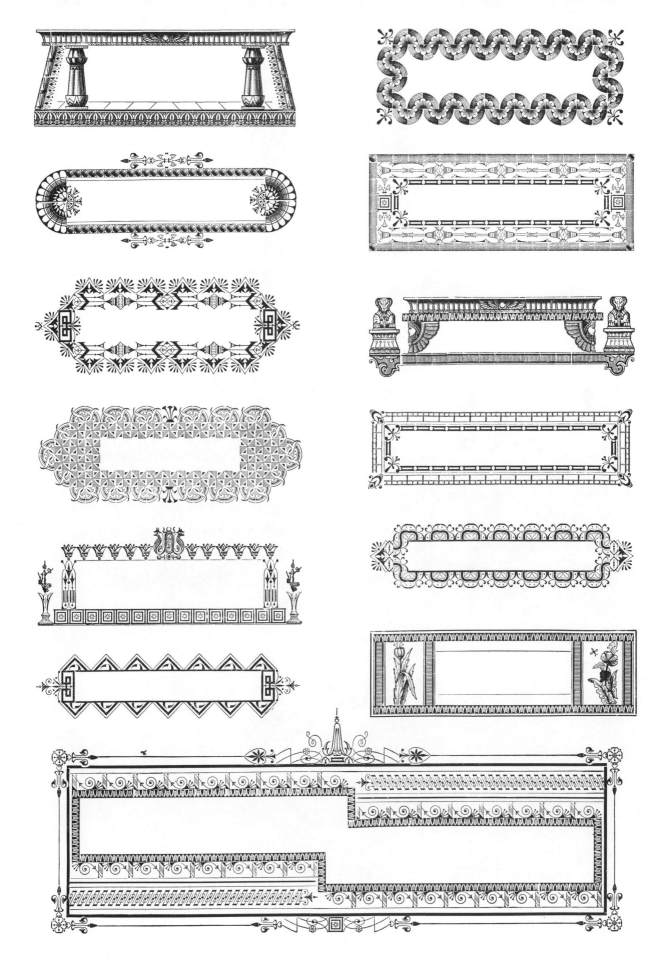

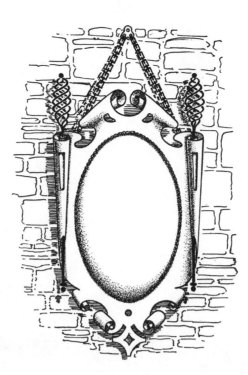

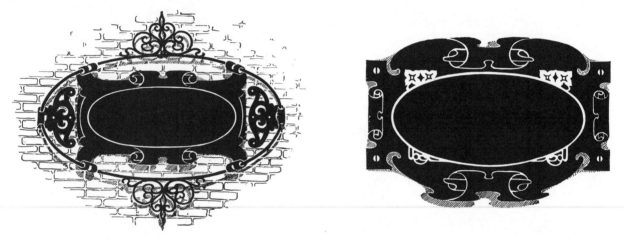

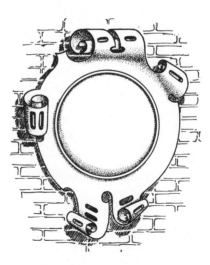

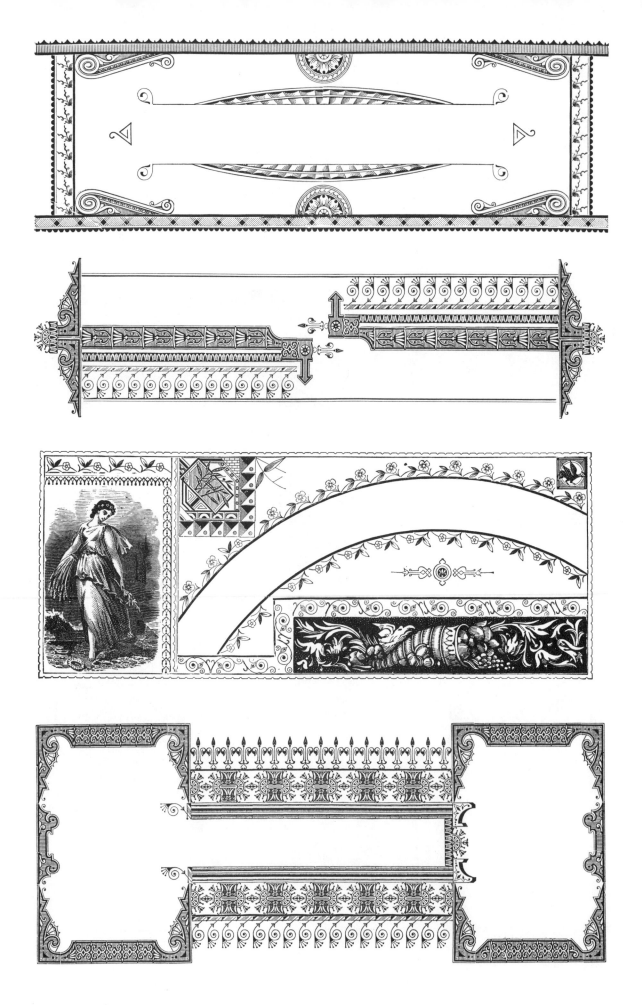

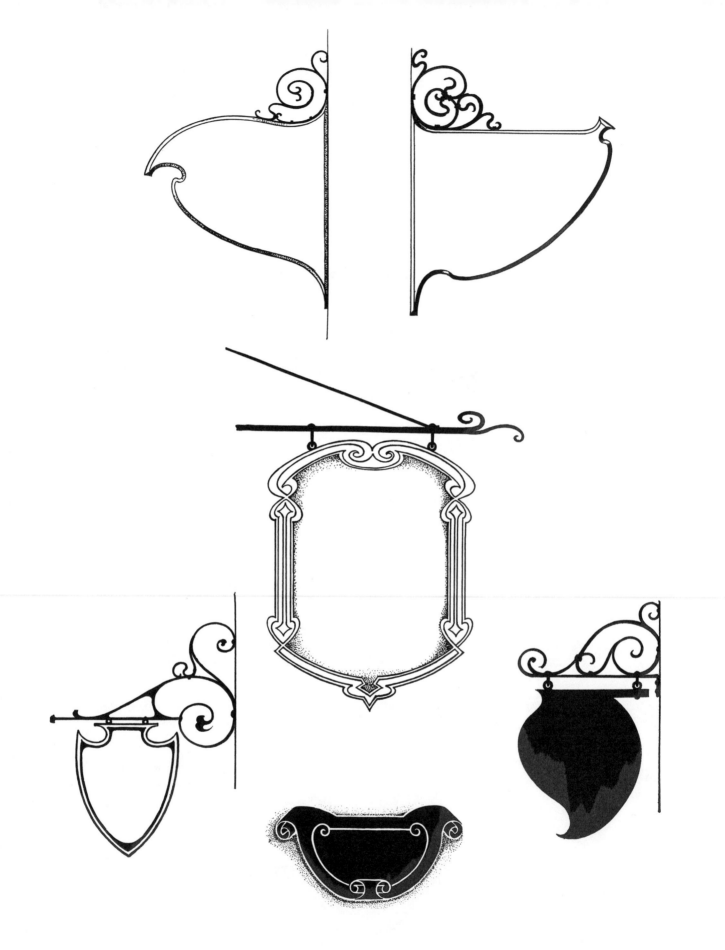

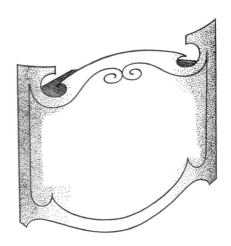
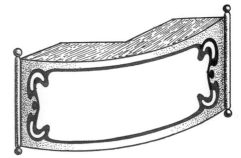
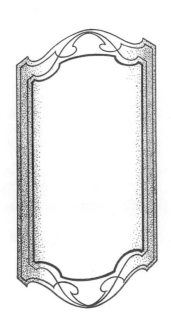
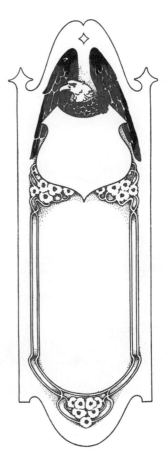

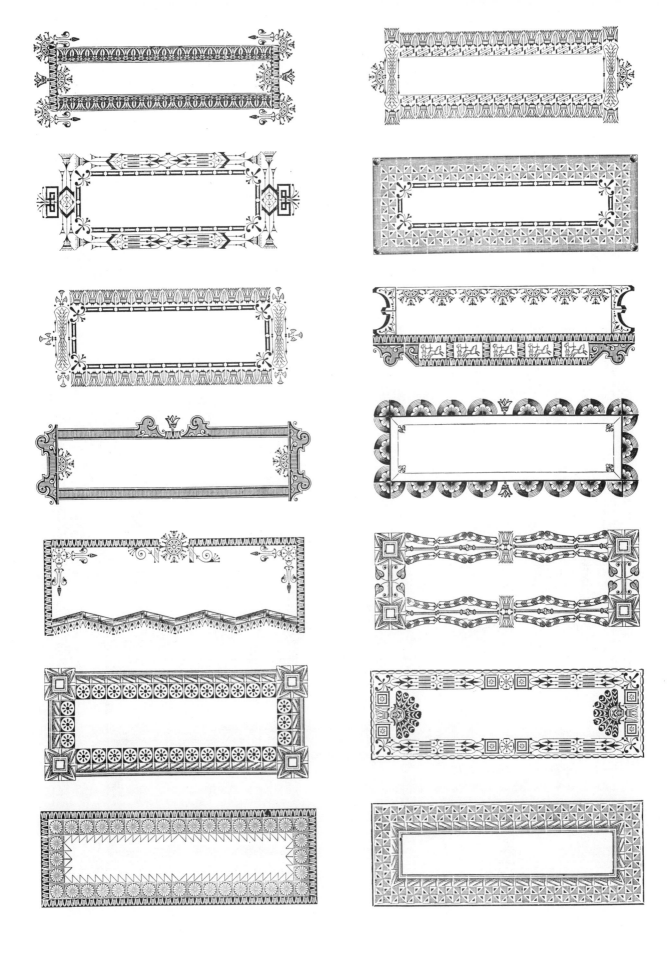

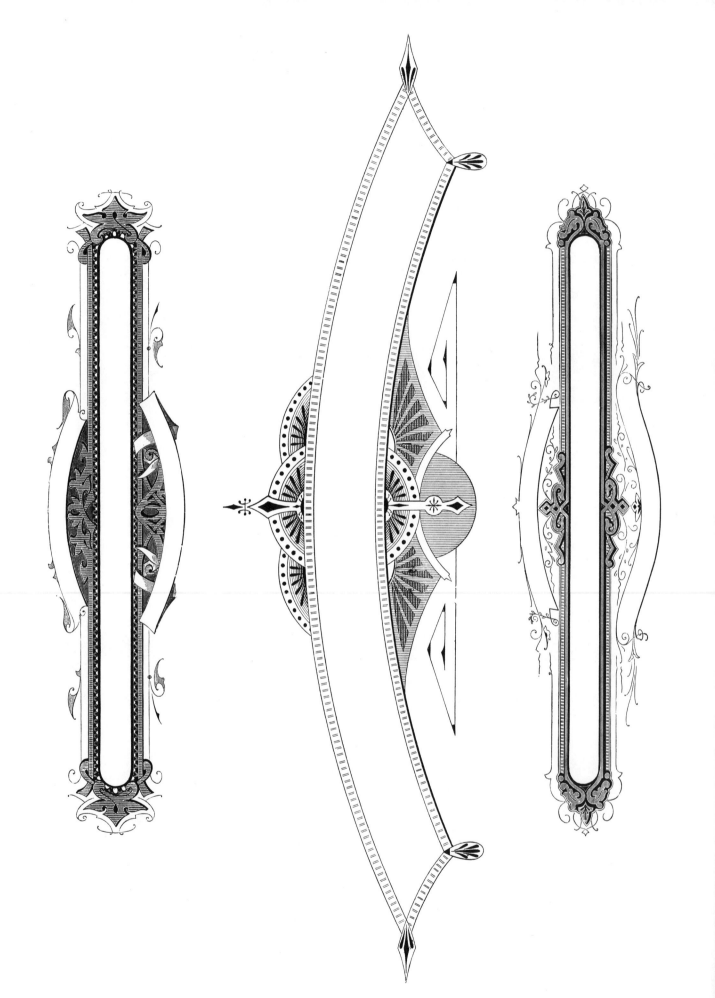

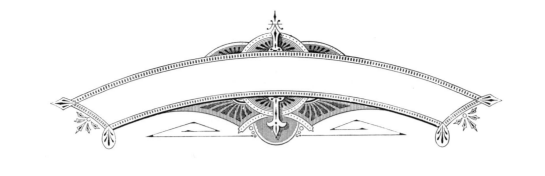

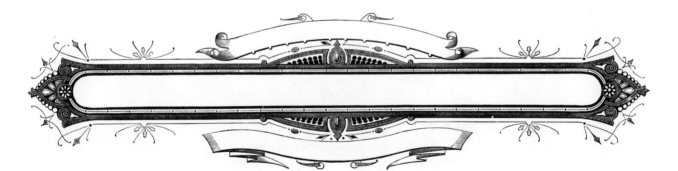

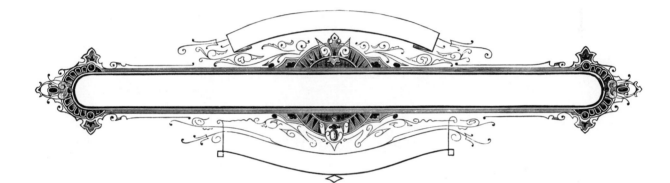

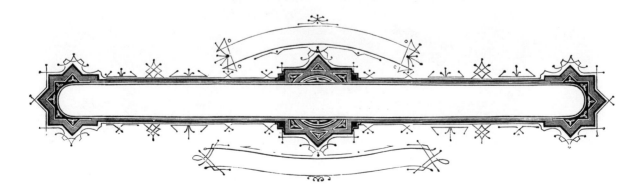

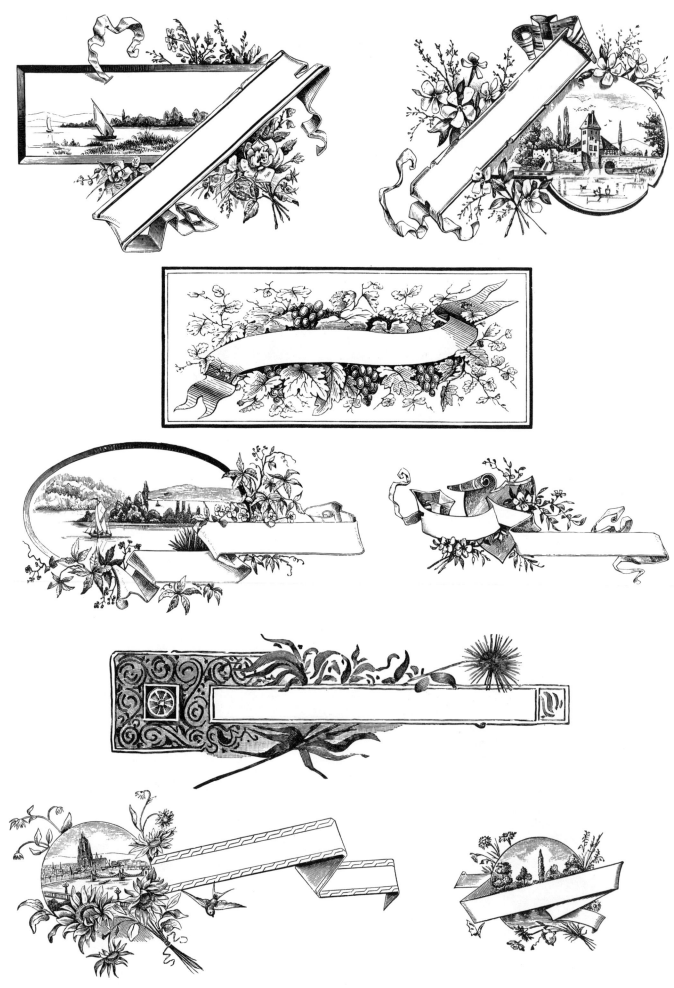

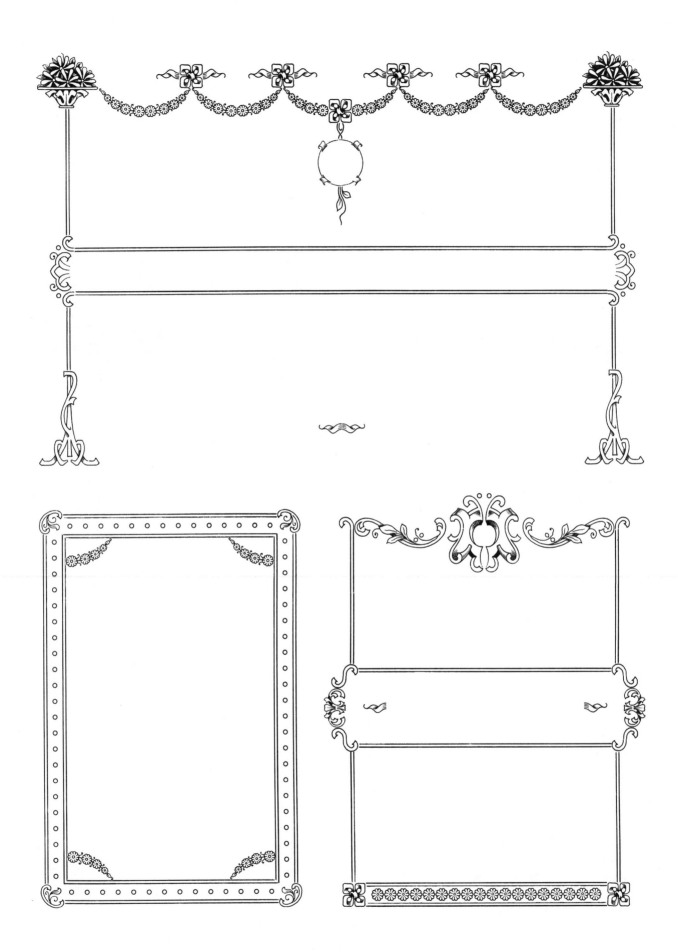

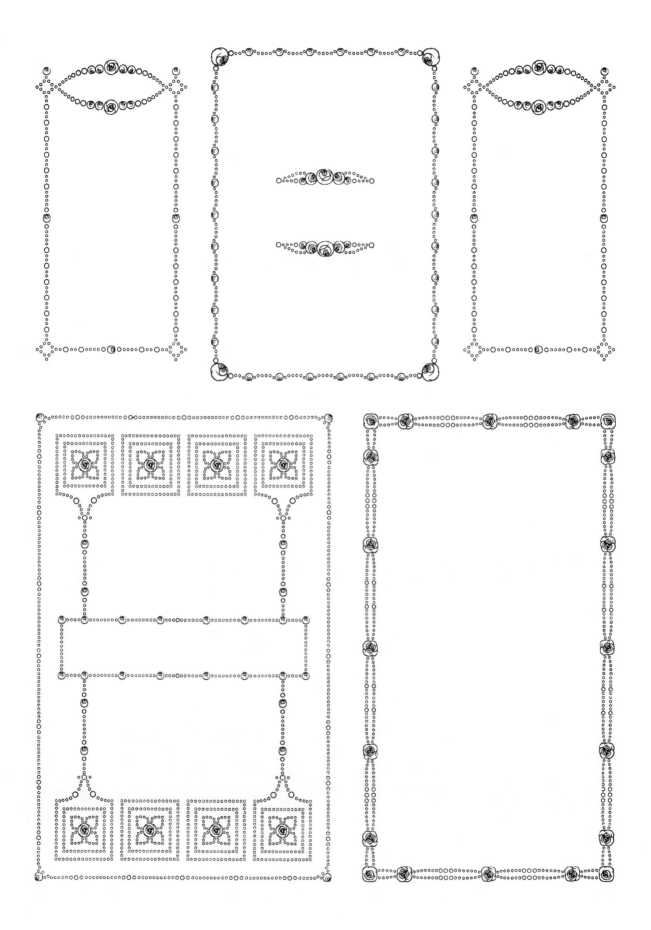

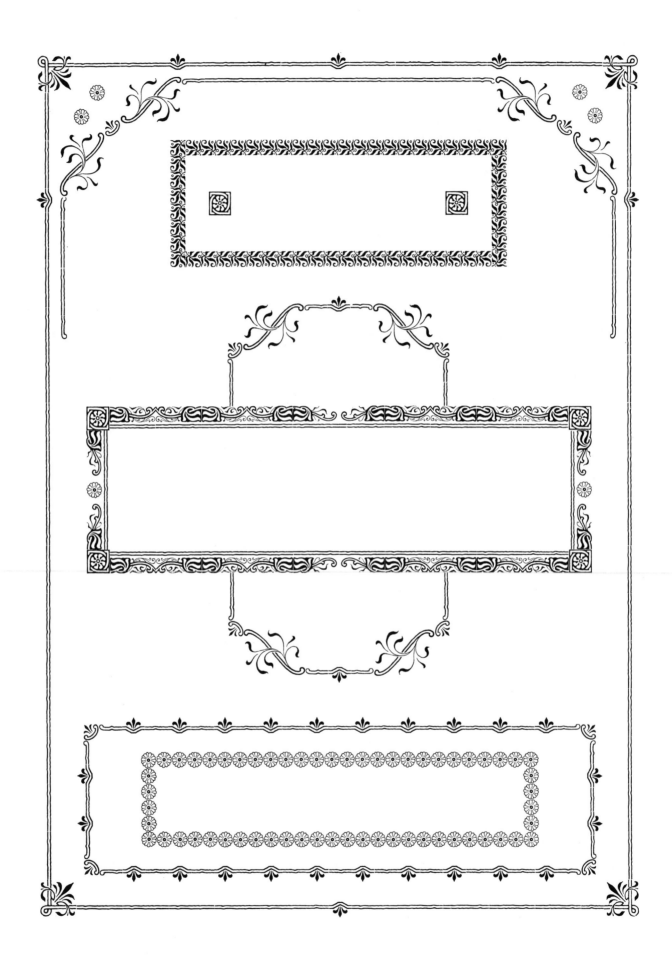

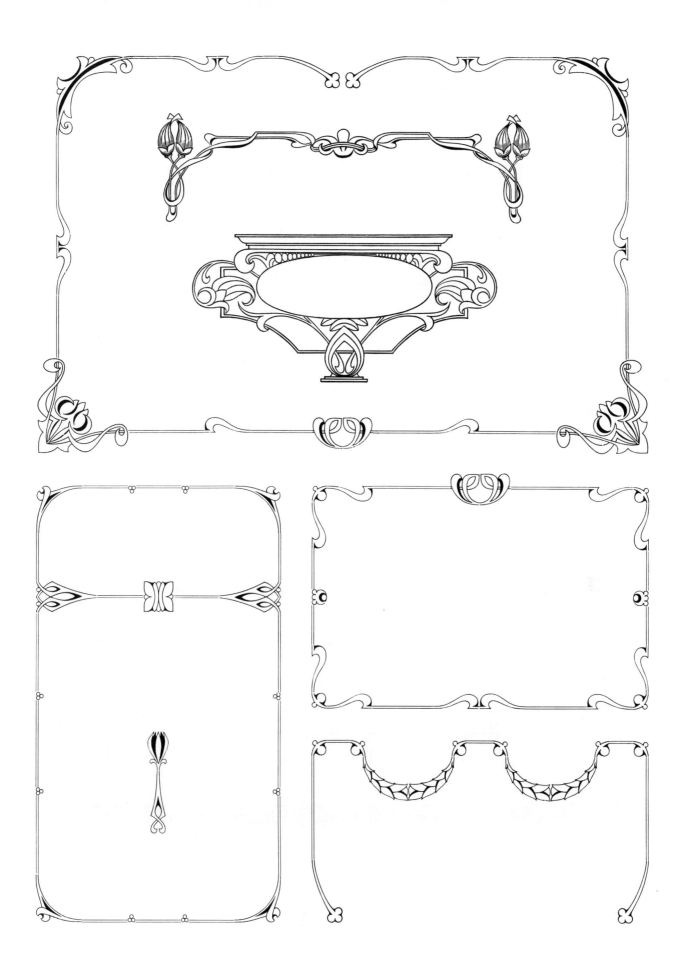

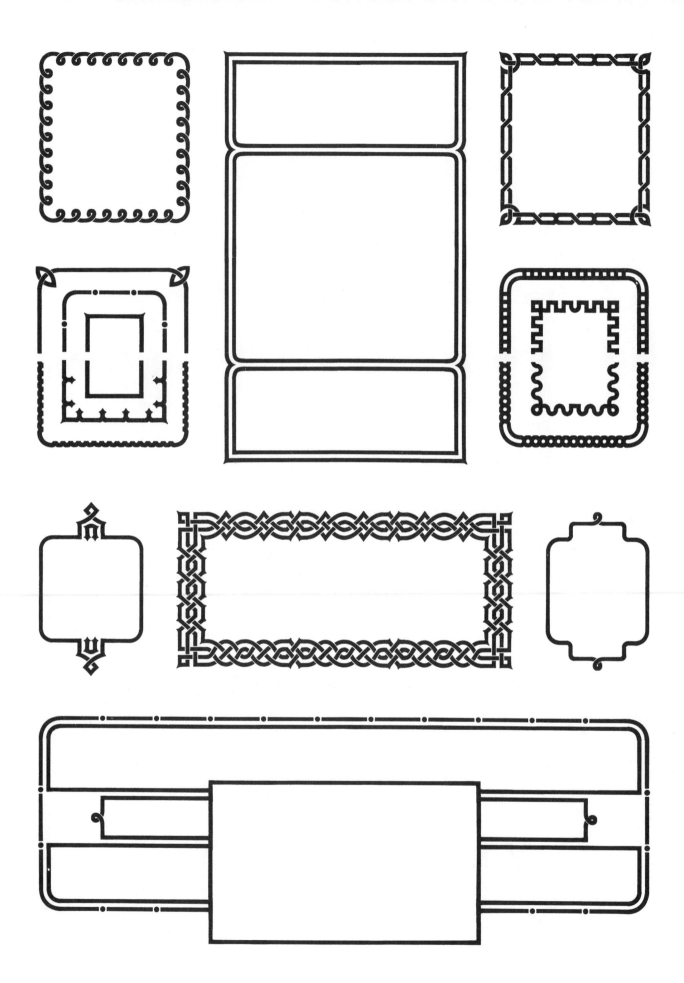

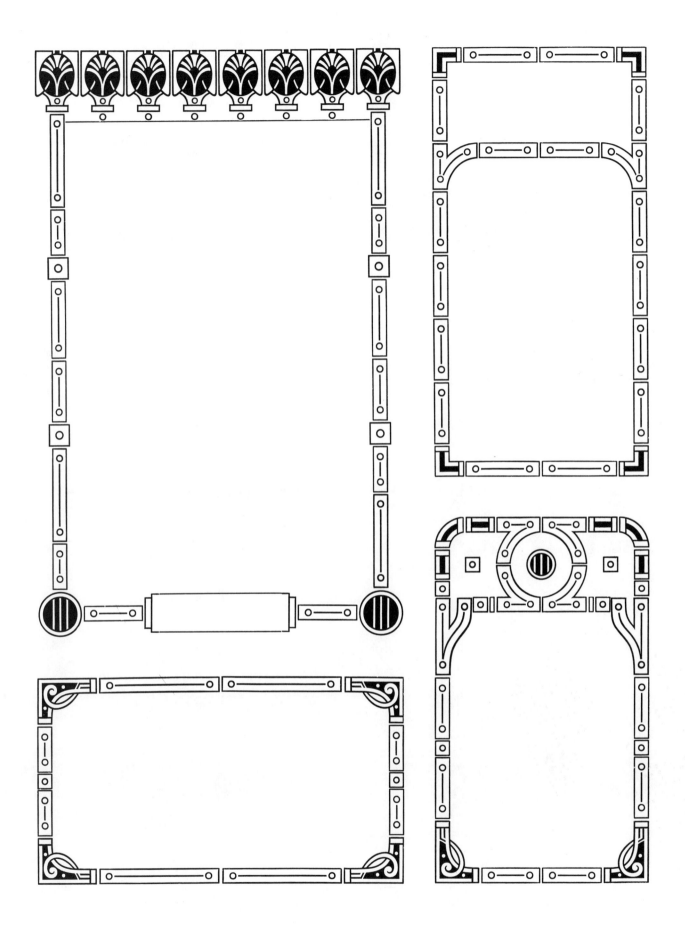

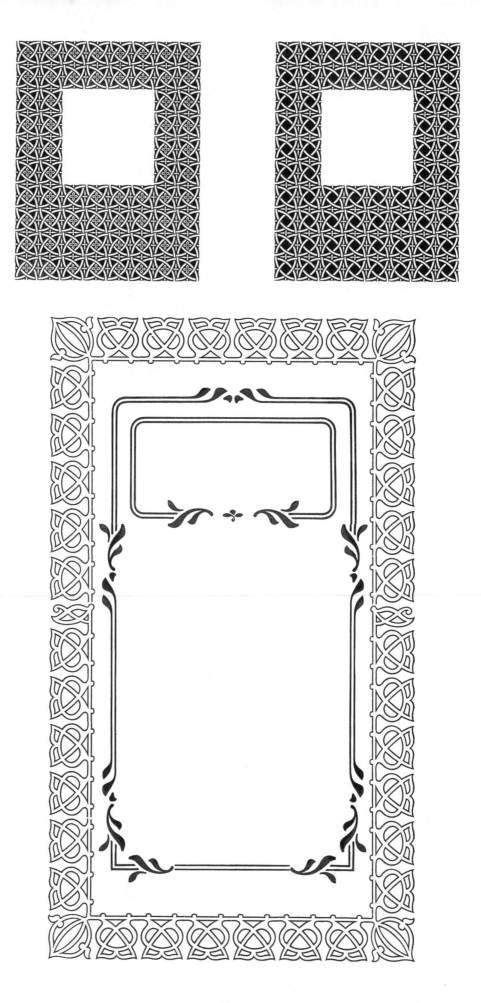

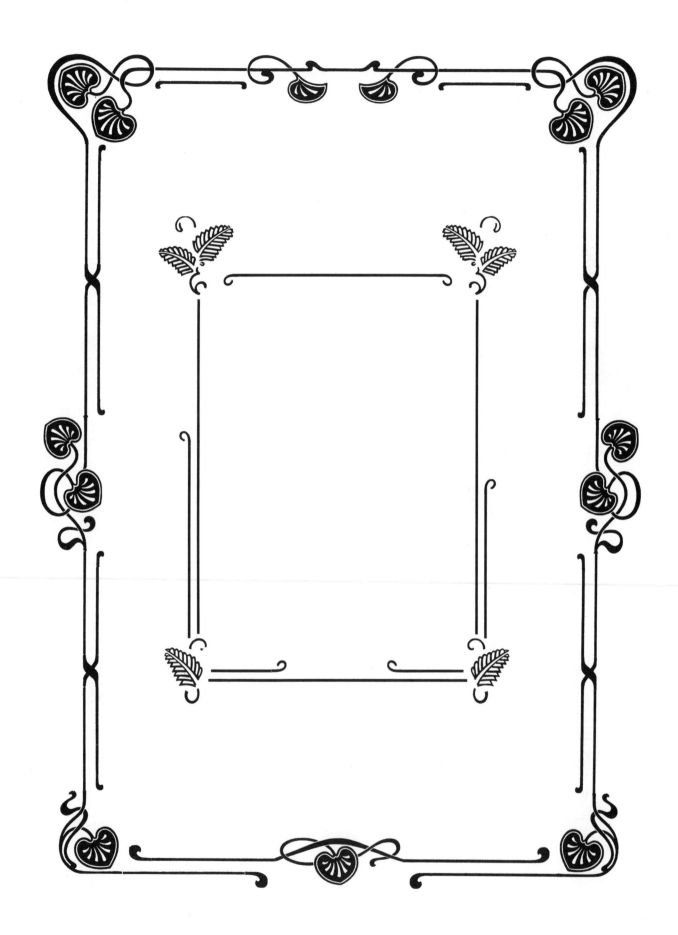

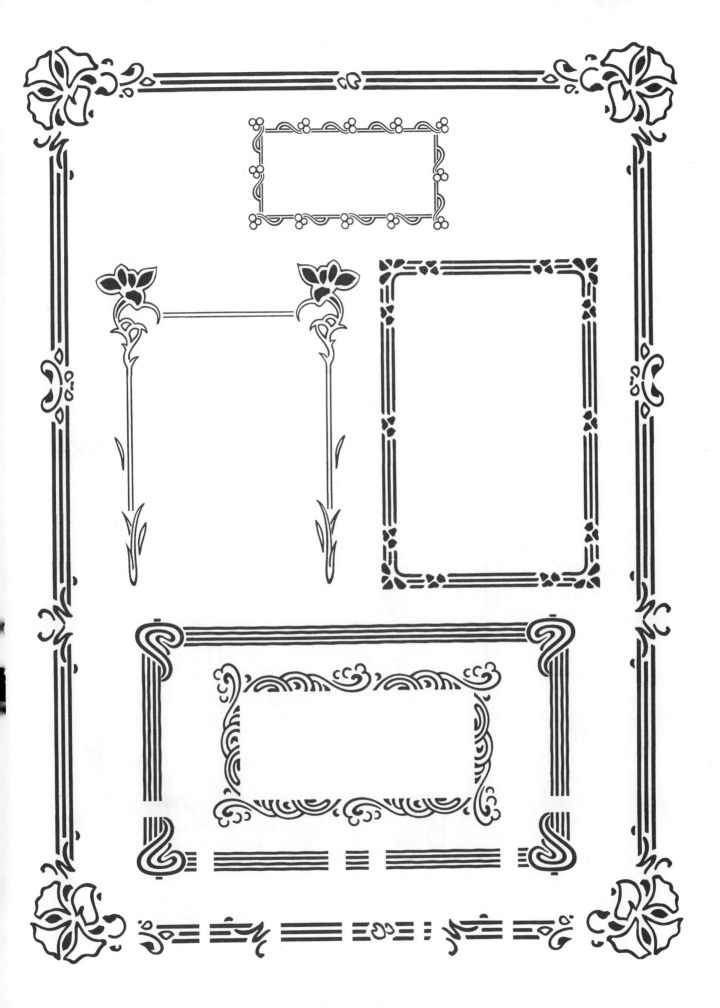

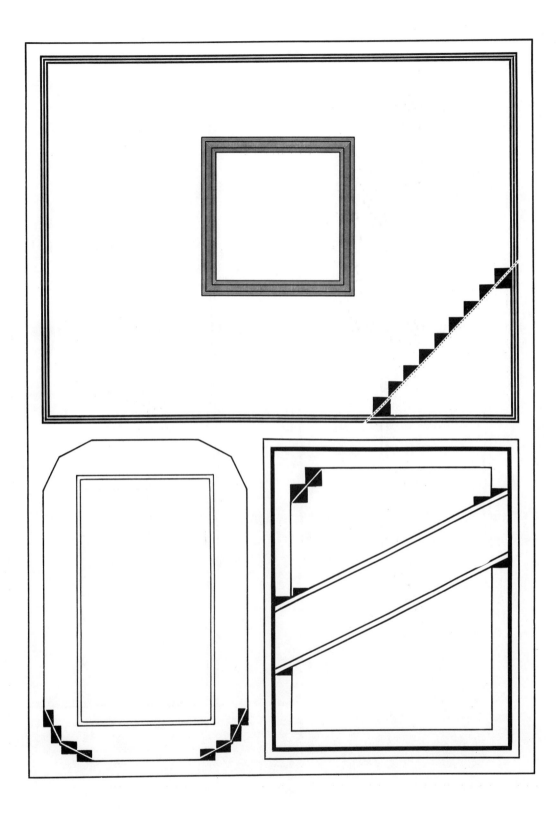

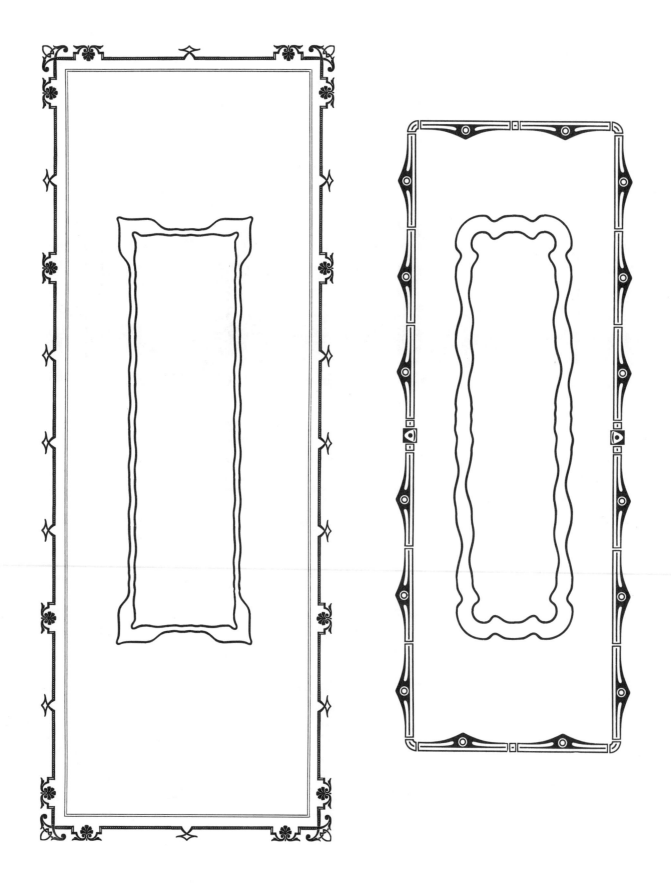

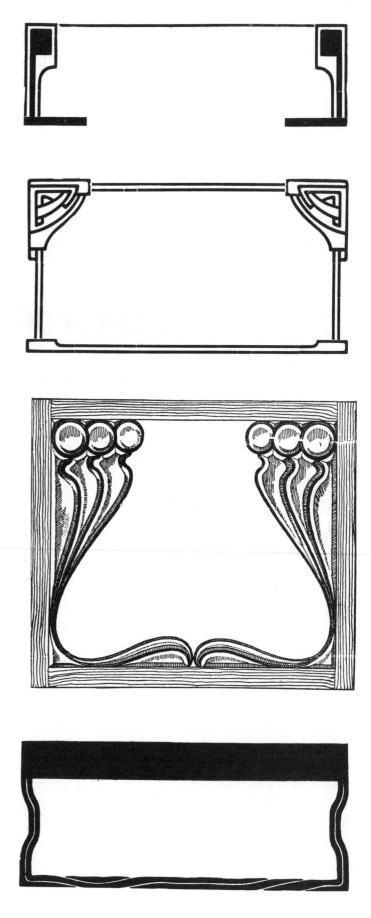

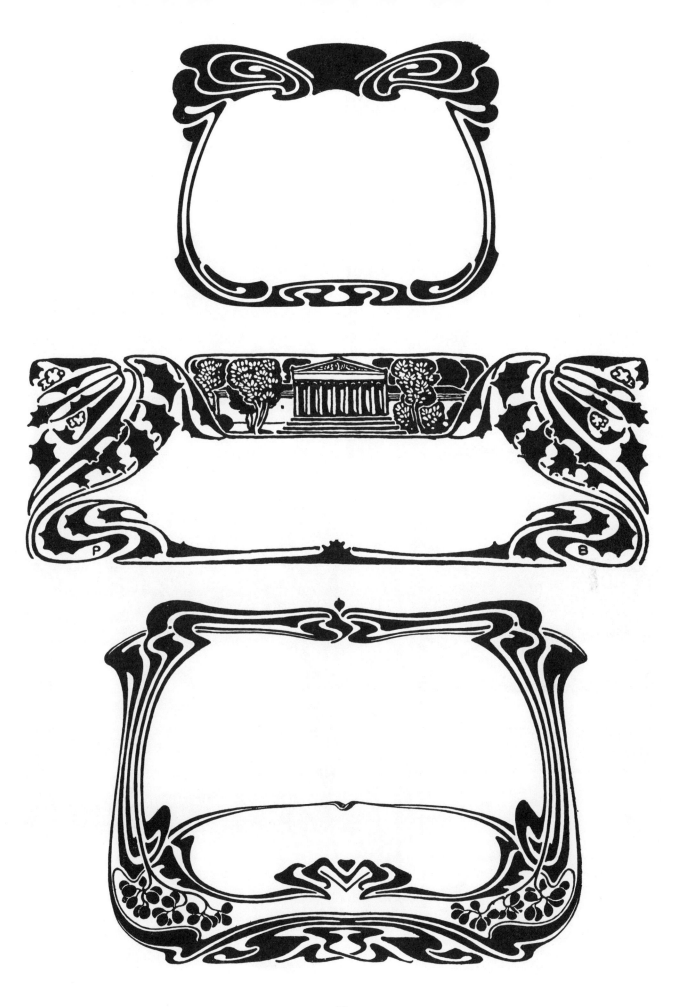

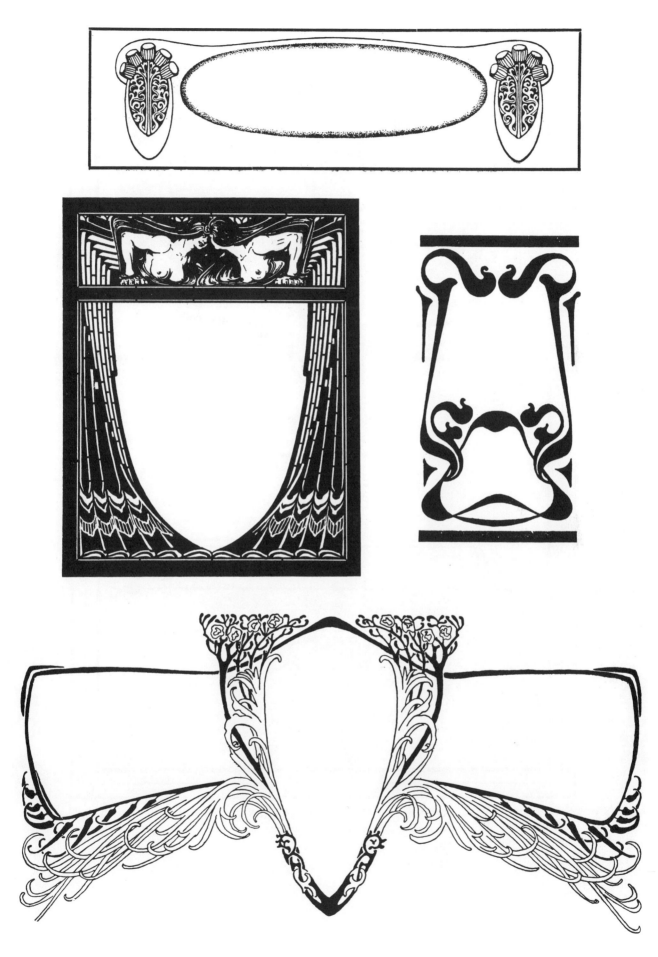

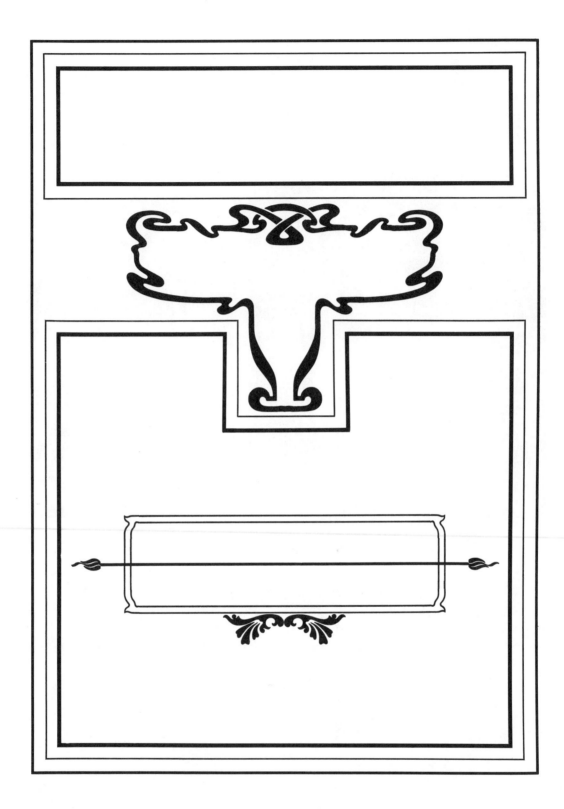

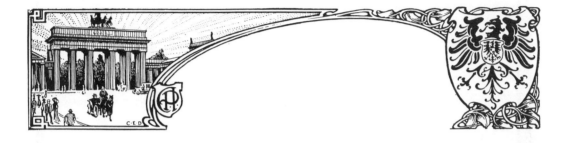

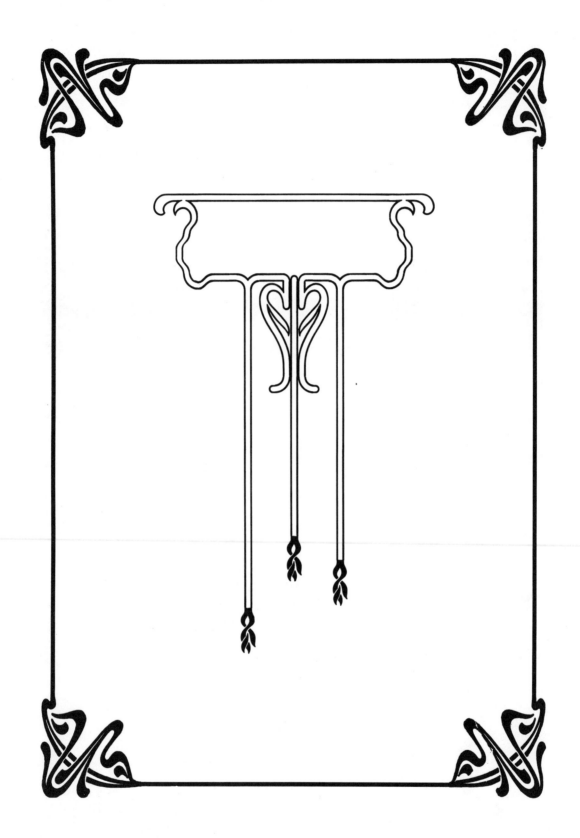

89

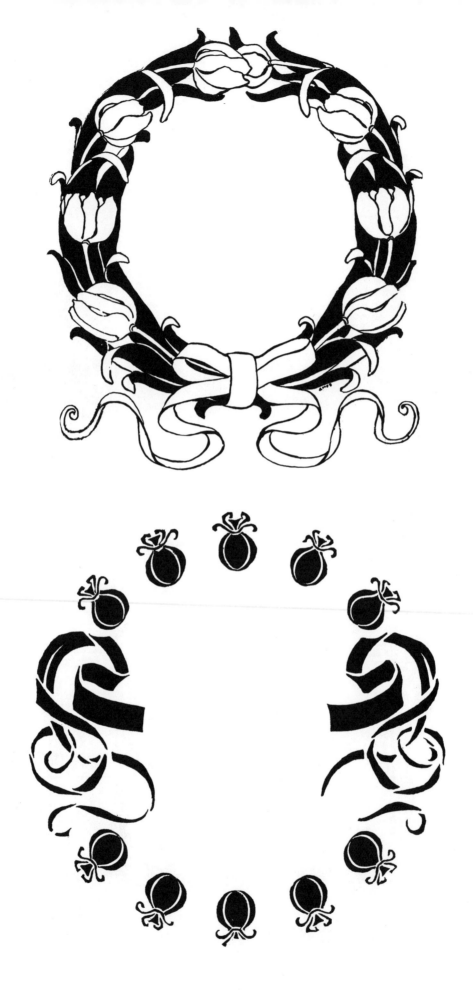

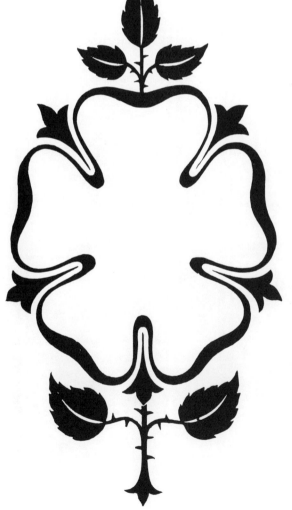

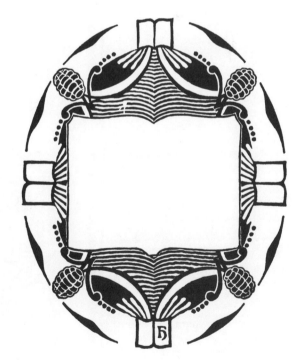

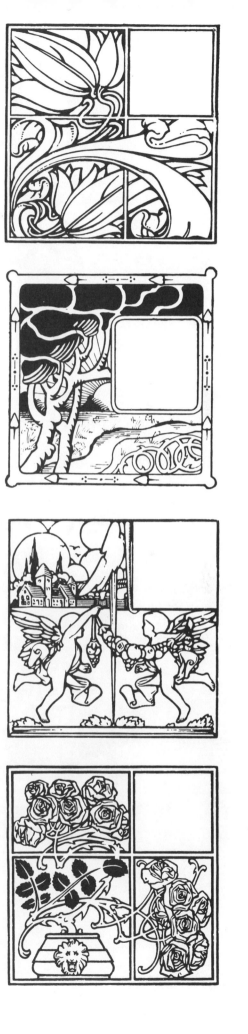

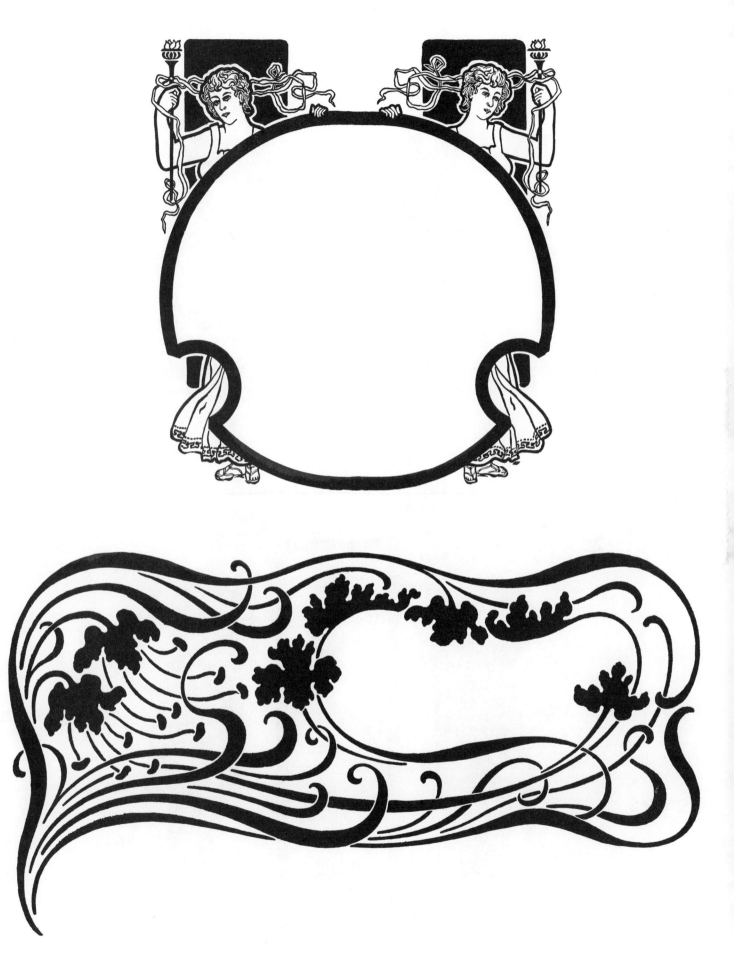

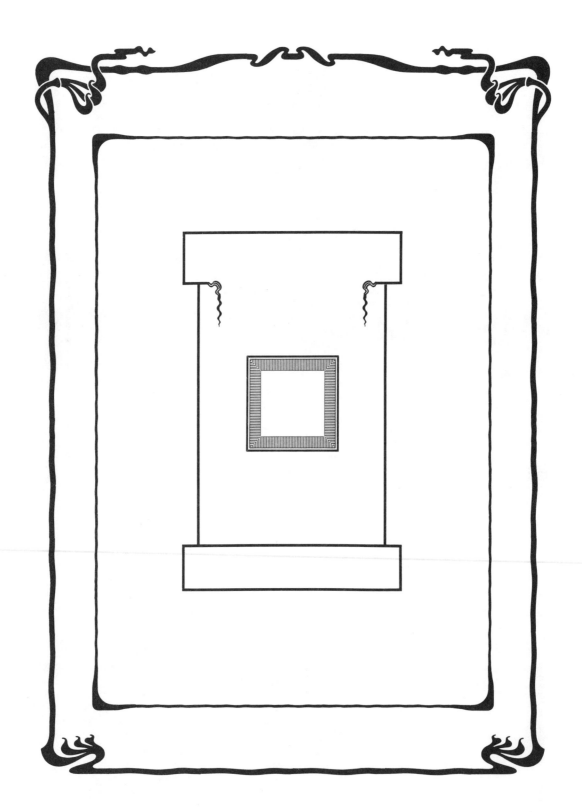

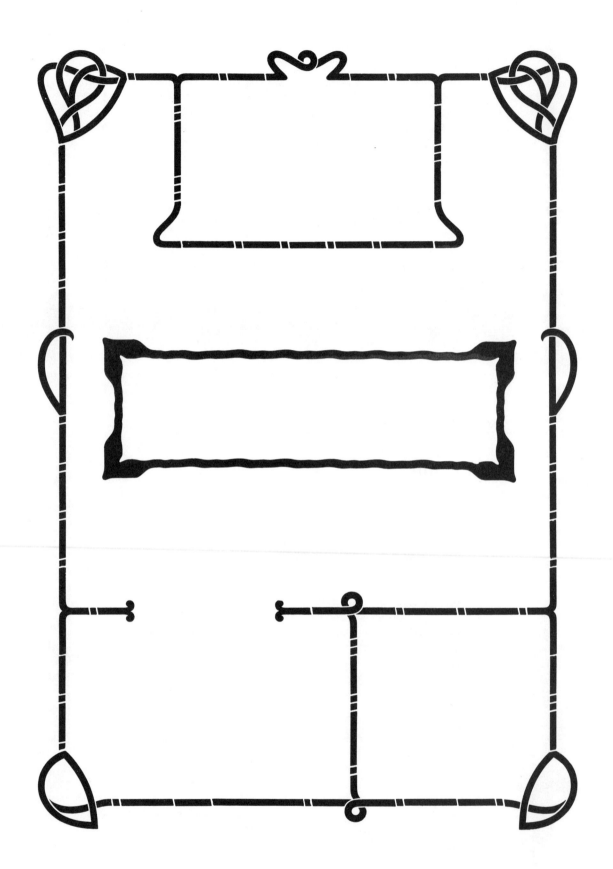

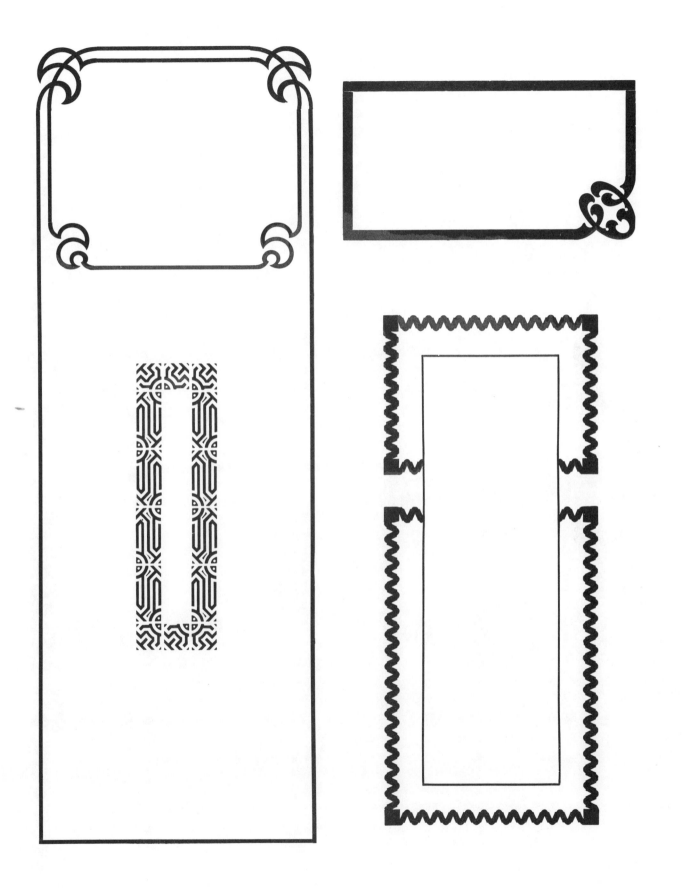

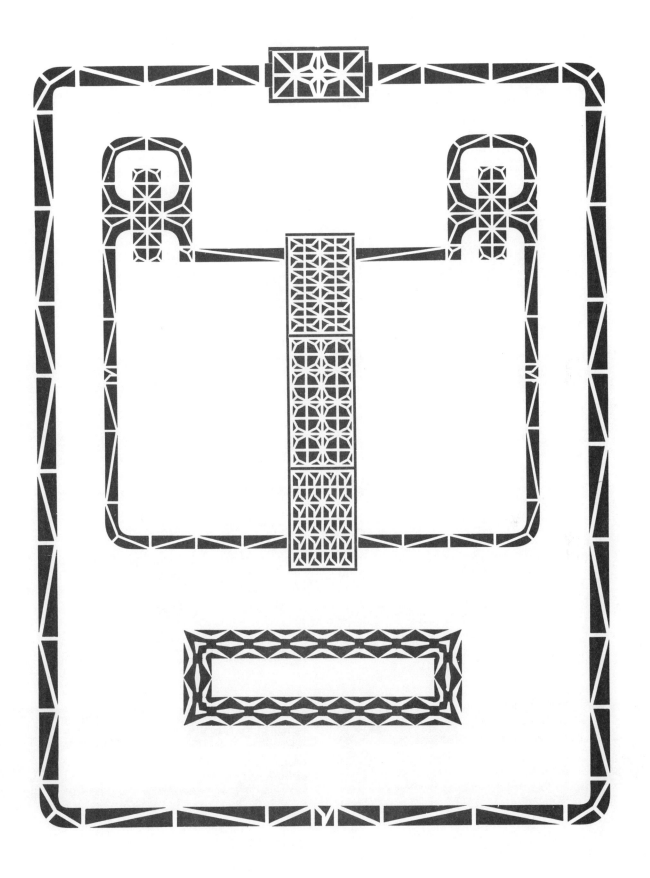

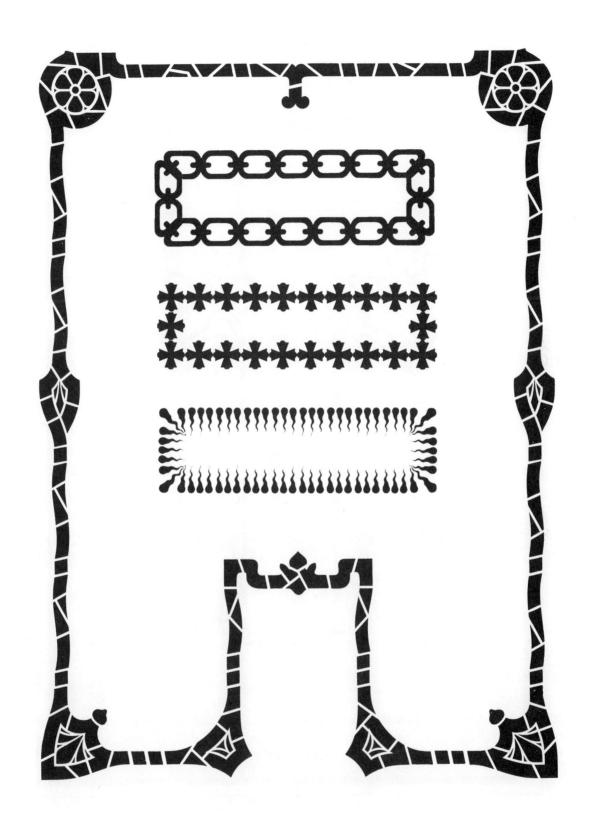

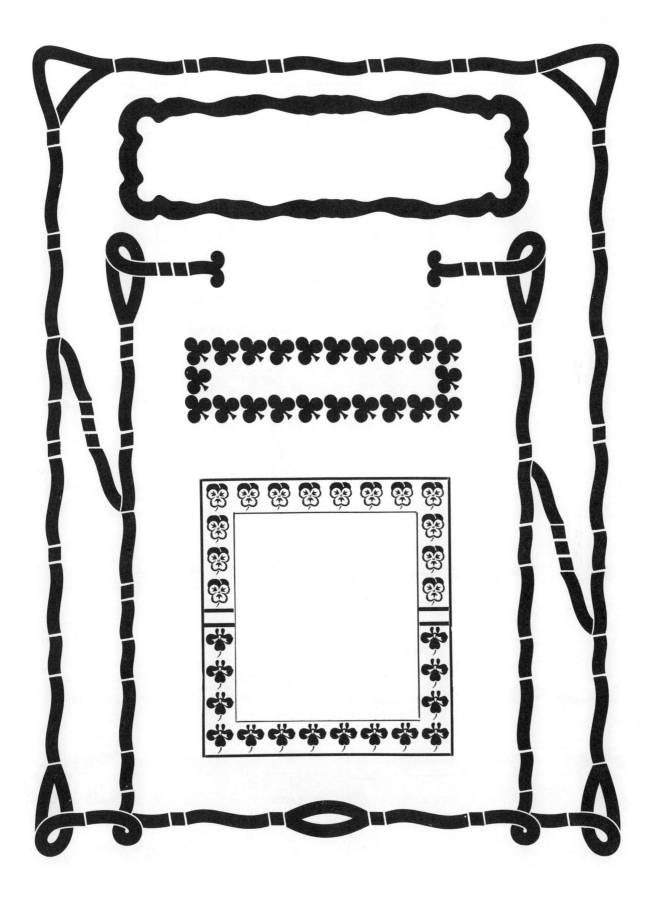

115

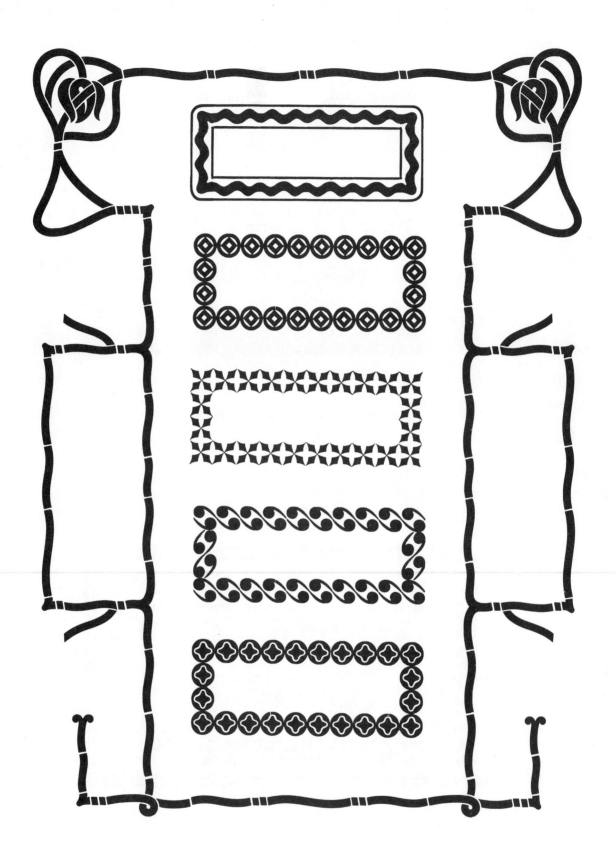